Meeting Saint Germain

Meeting Saint Germain

Wesley Adam Thomas

Meeting Saint Germain

Copyright © 2013 by Wesley Adam Thomas
www.MeetingSaintGermain.com

All rights reserved. No part of this book may be reproduced in any form or by any electronic or mechanical means including information storage and retrieval systems, without permission in writing from the author.

Shasta Clouds photo (front cover) by Emily Lynn
Interior design by River Sanctuary Graphic Arts

ISBN 978-1-935914-27-3

Printed in the United States of America

Additional copies available from:
www.riversanctuarypublishing.com
www.Meeting SaintGermain.com

River Sanctuary Publishing
P.O. Box 1561
Felton, California 95018
www.riversanctuarypublishing.com
Dedicated to the awakening of the New Earth

Meeting Saint Germain

Dedication

For my children
Sweetie and Bud

Acknowledgment

Kai,
my friend and editor

CONTENTS

1   **Portland, Oregon**
    1 We Meet
    13 The Higher Self
    19 Moving Days

2   **Mount Shasta**
    29 On the Mountain
    35 Ascension

3   **Shasta Valley**
    43 In the Valley
    47 The Shasta Valley Lessons
        47 Relationships
        48 Gain and Loss
        49 Thankfulness
        50 Healings
        51 Addiction
        53 Food
        54 Money
        55 Earth Issues

4 The Violet Flame
- 61 The Flame
- 67 The Order of the Violet Flame
- 73 Signing On for Service
- 75 Teachings
  - 76 The Divine Pilot Light
  - 78 Mystic Experience
  - 79 Returning to Earth
  - 80 Sharing Spirituality
  - 82 Balance
  - 83 The Word "God"
  - 84 Prayer
  - 86 "Unforgiveable" Actions
  - 88 Personal Devastations
  - 89 Suffering Abuse
  - 92 Fear
  - 93 Works
  - 95 Your Life Mission
- 98 Closing Comments

5 Afterword
- 103 The Book
- 107 Postscript
- 111 Benediction

Foreword

Call me Wesley. I'm a father, a teacher, a musician, a writer. After my divorce, the steady path to a comfortable retirement and old age disappeared, like a mountain trail abruptly ending in the bushes...when night's about to fall. In the confusion that followed, I looked within. I endeavored to "be still and know." In the silence came these pages.

At first I questioned the source of this material, never thinking of myself as someone Saint Germain would address. But setting those concerns aside, I continued writing. The document grew, and believing in its significance to myself and others, I eventually grew comfortable with the idea of channeling G, as he's sometimes called. As he once asked, "If the ideas are valuable and enlightening, what difference does the source make?"

I've never wished to be known as a New Age channel, even though traces of my experience come to light here. My idea of a perfect channel is someone like Geraldine Innocenti. She brought us thousands of pages from numerous ascended masters in *The Bridge to Freedom*; yet from reading that work, we have no idea who she is.

One difficulty I've had with metaphysical writings, however, is that they can be too ethereal. So in hopes of grounding this material, I've included some events from my personal journey and any advice from G that may be helpful to others.

Are there new concepts here? I don't think so. I've read hundreds of books on spiritual issues and these ideas all come up: meditation, channeling, karma, reincarnation, the higher self, the Violet Flame, ascension.

Nonetheless, until now, they haven't been presented in just this way, and it's my hope that *Meeting Saint Germain* will find its way to a fresh audience and expand awareness of the coming era.

—Wesley Adam Thomas

Mount Shasta, California
Spring, 2013

Portland, Oregon

Spring, 2009

We Meet

[A teacher of mine, Aurelia Louise Jones, once said to me that many mediums were just "channeling themselves." I've never been truly comfortable with the process. During the time these messages came, I often wondered if they were only my imagination. Saint Germain addressed these concerns during our early encounters.]

The lingering energies of meditation
have opened your hearing.
This is a small room,
but I'm standing about five feet away,
in front, to the right,
sharing space with the closet wall.

Nothing there stays:
the table, the notebook, the pen…your body.
The soul passes through these temporary forms
in search of enlightenment.

Continue your meditations,
for the mind discovers its source
by directing attention there.
I'll return, and as I've done with others,
I'll speak while you write.

Let's meet often…

Meeting Saint Germain

…You're here because I called you.
Don't you remember rustling about the kitchen,
thinking, "I'm ready to meditate now."
But then you got distracted with the dishes.
The timer sounded to signal the end of meditation,
but you hadn't even started.

So you came to this room and set the timer again,
but were fussing over some money schemes.
Finally you asked, "Why am I here?"
and that slowed you down.

Seeing an opportunity,
I approached around your right side,
toward your field of vision.
When I turned and looked,
your attention keened and now you are writing.

You'll find meditation and channeling
to be the most peaceful activities of the day,
and one who has peace needs little else.
Such tranquility is found only within,
but one must make time for it.

When you are inclined to meditate,
leave all and go to the altar.
Profound powers call homeward your soul.

Clinging to the material world
is the tragedy and waste of human life.

Embracing spirit sweeps one home to a glorious sun.
So turn away from the noise of everyday life;
the more time spent with beings of the higher realms,
the more grounded you'll be.

Is this not what you seek?
Peace of mind?
The noble love of others, and loving them as well?
Is this not your mission?
Returning home to where the heart was conceived?

I'm not the only ascended being available.
A community of risen souls
who have mastered the trials of human life
are now dedicated to helping others do the same.

We love you here, we want you near.
Your heart is precious to us.
We know you must complete the Earth studies,
but we are the discovery of those endeavors.

Your struggles have turned you toward us,
but their accompanying distress dims our presence.
In angry impatience you sometimes turn away,
but we never turn from you.

We call you always.
You are our child, our friend, our spirit.
No one on Earth loves you more…

…You were lonely and restless this afternoon,
nearly falling into the old patterns,
wasting the night in the city's worn-out bars.

But you stayed home
and discovered restlessness to be more edifying
than superficial activity.

You're being mindful, not drinking the nights away,
and this is your reward, to speak with us.

The evenings are what we've gained,
and these moments before sleep prepare you
for the dreams to come.

Sweet may they be…

…So often, the worldly and the spiritual conflict.

You blame yourself for not dedicating enough time,
for being too distracted by the needs of Earthly survival
to pursue the higher truths.

Rather than helplessly throwing up your hands,
work toward more poise.
What is a channel
but someone able to walk the border of two realms
and communicate with both.

If you wanted only to hear our messages,
you could have just stayed in our dimension,
but those already in the spirit realms
don't need the teachings;
those of the world do.

Expecting a steady state of bliss
channeling higher beings to a grateful world,
is sure to lead to disappointment.
We understand such a wish,
but our experience has revealed its limitations.
Honor this commitment as faithfully as your job.
The job keeps you on Earth,
and this work keeps you in the universe.

Spiritual activities produce a more efficient life.
Your personal affairs will then fall into place.
The laws of the universe are the ones to follow.

Others have dedicated more time to channeling
and more time to their worldly commitments,
but do what you can,
and don't worry about disappointing us.

We are making our own decisions
and bear some responsibility
for the results of addressing you.
As for now, we are pleased…

...You are ensconced in the family man,
the career man, the college teacher.
You've created a workable personality for the world,
and to some extent this is commendable.

Your householder days ended unhappily,
but consider if you'd have thrived in that role,
or whether the divorce opened unexpected opportunities.
As to your profession, so much of education
has been reduced to preparation for careers
rather than enriching the human experience.

The thousands of classes you've stood before
suggest your potential to be a way-shower.
Redirecting your energies to spiritual guidance
would not be a surprising change.

You must step forward, however.
You must offer guidance to those who want it.

Not all will be interested, or even supportive,
but theirs is another path.
May they find their way as well.

Nearly all channels have their doubts,
but they know whether or not they are imposters.
Some may accuse you,
but that is not in your power to change.

You know how you receive these words.
Yes, they are influenced by your personality,
your sense of language, and your interests,
but you hear them from us.

The best words flow with ease and grace.
When others write or speak so freely,
they are also channeling higher entities,
though they may not think so.

We know you are not one to impose your presence.
Though quiet and withdrawn,
think of the thousands of lectures given,
the hundreds of pages already written.

We don't ask anything unusual;
just change your presentations to address
      spiritual issues.
Speak well, speak assuredly,
have in mind the best interests of those you address,
and you will thrive…

…So, we meet again,
and we're glad you've responded to our call,
however off-schedule we may be.

A productive writing session now
will encourage future encounters.
Our rendezvous are sometimes inconvenient

but the writings will be better for it.
We're happy you've taken them on.
May they bring a new voice to our message.

Did you notice your restlessness late last night?
A previous dinner discussion
had you up and thinking at 2:00 a.m.
despite your early morning classes.

You had avoided talking about these pages.
Although this fear should pass with time,
it can become entrenched and difficult to weed out,
so learn to trust others.

Those who know of your previous channelings
should not be surprised.
Begin by telling them.

At times you worry about your teacher's warning
that some mediums are only channeling themselves,
but if so, what of it?
If the ideas are valuable and enlightening,
what difference does the source make?

Do you feel it presumptuous
that "little ole you" claims to channel
the "high and mighty" Saint Germain?
That I am supposedly "high profile"
makes it *more* likely you'd hear me, not less.
As I've said to others,

we laugh when we are put on pedestals.
We are workers, and we speak to all who listen.

Nothing in these writings is pretentious.
No one is forced to read.
Leave these doubts aside and plunge into the work.
Now on with you.

I defer to your guides, so honorable and respectful.
They may seem less present than before, but not so.
They step aside and let you live,
knowing that the Earthly trials develop the soul.

Truly, you are in such beautiful spiritual company…

…When you wonder whether to interrupt a meditation
and yield to an inclination to write,
I say explicitly, "Yes, you should."

Meditation is important, certainly,
but when you feel pressure on your right palm,
I am present and ready to speak.
Record my words, for I may not always be so near.

How will these teachings be revealed
unless brought forward by those who hear them?
If those who know don't speak,
discussions will be led by those who don't know…

...Trust these communications.
Don't ask whether you are just imagining them,
or whether the thoughts are of any value.

Such questions are devices of the mind.
They may help with mundane matters of the world,
but here we deal with faith.

The third dimension operates on certain premises
over which humans are given some dominion,
but when you direct attention toward us,
leave some of those Earthly disciplines behind.

Others may be doubtful, but that is their rational mind
challenging truths that are beyond rationality.
I am here speaking;
besides these words, what proof do you need?

You continue to wonder
why I would speak to someone as "low profile" as you,
but to us, everyone matters.
We of the higher realms speak to thousands.
We desire as many voices on Earth as possible,
every one of them precious.

You need but listen and write.
Don't worry about how this work will be received.
Your responsibility is only to present it.
The underlying truths will eventually be accepted,
for all are embodied souls with a spiritual heritage...

...All are worthy of my attention,
but those ready to turn from the world of form
and seek the inner realms
are more open to my message.

Like you, they often begin a spiritual quest
in response to a personal devastation,
discovering that their life in the third dimension
is too limited for the powerful being that is their soul.

Were I to speak directly to all people,
many would question their own perceptions
and discredit my voice.

Some will accept and express my messages to others.
As channels, they bring their own habits,
but I work with their personal inclinations
and communicate through them.

Yes, the channel flavors the message, as they say,
but these drinks are mixed in holy water,
so serve them.

You're not a lunatic abandoning the rational world.
You're one of many pioneers preceding the millions
who'll join us in the higher realms.

I've lived many lives
and confronted your same concerns.
I'm no longer timid about sharing my knowledge,

nor should you be,
for no one can deny others their beliefs.

Those walking the spiritual path ask fear to step aside.
Your soul is not afraid or defeated or tired or fallen.
It blazes with magnificent force.

Does the spine slump, straighten it.
Do the shoulders droop, lift them.
Break through the egg;
leave the shell to the ashes of time,
and awaken the phoenix inside.

How far behind your doubts will someday seem.
How far ahead you'll fly,
eyes lifting with the rising soul,
and as you ascend may the winds in your wake
lift others as well.

The Higher Self

[Saint Germain often spoke of the higher self. I've gathered passages from those sessions and present them here.]

You have a healthy body, but it is not you.
Wesley is not you.
Your job is not your mission.
Your pleasures are not your passions.
The sights you see are not your life vision.

A spiritual being probes the world through you.
Still and strong in an unknown place,
it observes your earthly experience,
assessing you as a builder considers a tool.
Does the tool work?
Does it accomplish the expectations of the builder?
Or if not, what *can* it accomplish?

Wesley provides one of many lenses
through which this presence
has experienced the third dimension.
When Wesley is done, this higher self continues.

When you come to Shasta this summer,
you may hear this called the *I Am* presence.
Until individuals detach themselves from the world,
quiet their minds, turn their attention inward,
and recognize this presence within,
spiritual progress is forestalled.

It is the kernel of ascension to the higher realms…

…Similar to a playwright doing a character sketch,
the higher self plans an Earth life.

You arrived with a healthy body,
an insightful intellect, an easy-going way,
and a disposition toward reading and writing.

Others have their own designs:
innate capabilities, talents, virtues, and preferences
chosen by their higher selves.

Writers will often notice, while creating a play,
that characters seem to have a mind of their own,
developing in unexpected ways.
Likewise, once a life begins, humans exercise free will.
They make their own decisions,
determining the effectiveness of their original plan.

A play is presented within a certain time limit,
restricted to a stage.
The drama involving you and your contemporaries
might have the working title *Comes A New Age*.

After the play is presented,
an author may reconsider a character,
keep some qualities, discard some, add others,

even create another role for another production.
The higher self sends a stream of lifetimes to Earth
to work on certain spiritual attributes;
this is how actions and experiences of former lives
influence the current personality.

The free will of humans is the unpredictable element.

From the viewpoint of those now living,
inexplicable events happen, life seems unfair,
or people may seem not to be created equal.

However, they all are souls undergoing Earth-training.
Their capabilities and dispositions are predetermined
by their higher selves' desire for spiritual progress…

…Well may you write,
for the channels are opened
by an appeal to your higher presence this morning.
Therein lies a well of spiritual strength.
When spirit is strong, life goes well.

Invoking your *I Am* presence
opened you to the higher dimensions.

Always connect with your inner power,
your personal source of divinity,
before calling upon those of us here….

…You nearly walked by the writing desk this morning,
but happily you sat down, arranged some blank pages,
and pulled a pen from the drawer.

The everyday world distracts channels.
They set spiritual activities aside,
feeling too busy or tired,
caught in the claptrap of day-to-day demands.

At times, spiritual well-being seems unrelated to life,
but viewing it as separate can cause difficulties.
Devote more of your life to the spiritual
and the division becomes less pronounced.

The spirit requires fewer physical resources,
for it is sustained by the divine presence
that created the material realm.
Connecting with your higher self
lifts you above the interplay of physical necessities.

Notice how life has changed
since you've considered your higher presence.
You've broken your routines, changed your diet,
planned your journey to Shasta,
and experienced the peacefulness
of listening to the inner promptings of the soul.

This all comes from seeking the source of your being.
You did not begin as a result of human conception.
You chose your parents in a higher reality,

as you've done many times before,
and as you master life on Earth,
as you clear karma,
you'll rejoin your higher self…

…Spiritual growth is like the salmon's journey.
Hatched in the shallow beds of a brook,
the smolt follow the stream
to the powerful currents of the river,
then to the vast ocean
of language and thought that comprise the adult ego.
In the prime of their maturity and power,
salmon hear a call home.

They leave the ocean behind,
swim back to the rivers,
up the streams,
spawning in the very brooks where they hatched,
and the same journey awaits the newborn…

…The supplications you made this morning
are true to the source.
They take you inward to your divine presence.
From there the heavenly energies
flow through you onto Earth.
Your readings and writings are important,
but you must take time to "be still and know."

Do any of your studies
bring the contentedness of this morning's meditation?
They point the way, yes,
but until you stop reading,
look inward, and invoke your higher self,
the experience is intellectual.
The meditation, however, is energetic:
you change physically.
The atoms of your body are cleansed by
a sweep of higher forces,
raising you from the chair.

When you stand and arch your arms upward,
lifting your face to the skies,
you are the tree of life,
receiving the divine energies
in an open posture of blossoming and growth.

Your mind emerges from meditation uncluttered,
functioning with the primal creative energies.
As these become your staple,
you'll join us in the higher realms.

Seek your own source of divinity, your higher self,
and encourage others to seek theirs.

This is the way of the wise.

Moving Days

[June found me stumbling about my possessions in a chaotic apartment. Moving this, donating that. Discarding this, recycling that. I decided to go "homeless" for the summer and set up camp on Mount Shasta.]

What to keep. What to let go. How to let it go.
These are major issues of life itself,
not just a man leaving an apartment.

You may resent the material possessions
but they did not ask to be acquired,
nor do they ask to be retained.
What are *you* ready to let go?

You may say, "All of it,"
and as a younger man you'd probably have done so,
but alas, decades of accumulation surround you.

In the moves since the divorce, you've let much go,
so acknowledge the progress you make with joy.

Sages so wise have held onto so little,
some only a loincloth and rice bowl.
Still, they have managed to fulfill life's purpose:
progress spiritually and help others do the same.

Don't agonize over what to keep or let go.
In time it is all going, including your body.
Live close to the soul; it stays.

In becoming one with God,
nothing of you remains.

Your job is but to make the journey…

…Let burn the candles and be with us awhile.

We know your life is transitioning.
Preoccupied with leaving this city,
you've set aside our sessions.

When you are too busy to meditate or channel,
you only delay an inevitable return to those activities.
Nothing serves you better;
no stronger source of power is available,
but you must do your share of the work.

These practices cleanse your aura,
clearing way for the higher energies and our voices.
You become more alert,
and current concerns are seen in perspective.
Then is a good time to listen and write.

So, apply yourself. Give spirit a chance…

…You are a worldly channel
with a suppressed desire for the spiritual,
but the truth will come forward,
through those quiet lips,
from these pages yet unseen.

Often, you dread disapproval of this work,
not so concerned that the writings are valid
as that others will belittle you.
Keep in mind that Jesus was not silenced
even by crucifixion,
a level of reproach you're unlikely to encounter.

Someday, you'll trumpet the truth
and your current reticence will seem a distant memory
of someone known in the past.

Your dedication to spiritual growth will transform
into a concern for the progress of others,
a sign of maturity and drawing closer to God.

One way or another, the soul will draw you near,
peacefully or more urgently.

As for now, we are pleased.

Do come to Shasta this summer, for we've much to do.
The sacred energies here
will more effortlessly bring this work together…

…Well *have* you thought of the adventure?
Of how unpredictable and surprising
a life devoted to spirituality would be?

Here you are, having left for work fourteen hours ago,
yet after the drive home and a quick dinner,
you're in the meditation room writing.

This is the type of energy such work brings.
It is interesting, inspiring, enticing.
The more you give it, the more it returns.
The more others receive, the more you'll want to offer.

Who will you meet along the way?
Where will the journey take you?
What destinations call?
What wonders wait?
When have you felt this way about *any* work?

…Come my son, I drag you by the arm from the bed.
It's late, but as often happens after spiritual studies,
you began to glow. This means you are close to truth.
It shines within you, triggered by your studies.

Great spiritual works direct readers inward
to the hearts with which they were born,
their unfettered hopes, their hidden treasures.

Can you not remember the freshness of childhood?
The world's sparkling details,
the unrestrained joy and hope?
They are still there
and re-approaching them is your journey home.

I believe you are less sleepy than when I roused you,
but I wish you sweet dreams.

I leave you to the comfort of your books and bed…

…We should speak tonight,
for again you've had a day of restless doubt.

You shouldn't worry that you are withdrawn.
Many spiritual leaders have lived alone in caves,
hermits known only to a few followers.

You *like* privacy and solitude.
You haven't been shunned or abandoned.
You often *choose* to avoid personal involvements.

These midlife years may not be what you planned,
but what is this unease?
That you are wasting time?
That the work here is a sign that you've "lost it?"

You must trust your perceptions.
Yes, you'll need guidance at times,
but you have the best counselors available, us.

You've chosen a less traveled path,
but others do take it, and it does lead somewhere.

Now off to bed with you.

Things will look better tomorrow…

…We're glad you've resumed daily meditations.
With each moment, the cares of the world dissipate,
and you stand tall and strong,
a white soul with a violet sheen.

Swept into vivid visions and imaginings,
pulsating with colorful lights,
your presence is quite easy to detect from here.

The place you now leave has been healing.
Upon sound advice,
you left the painful environs of a broken marriage
and moved to a location that had no history for you.

Continuing the spiritual studies will help as well,
offering a new commitment in a new
       spiritual community,
unencumbered by past paradigms of who you are.

What better place to go than Shasta?
For there on a high meadow
we once offered public knowledge of the New
    Golden Age.

Universal energies pervade the Mountain.
She is one of Earth's chakras,
receiving cosmic energies from all dimensions,
offering peace and reassurance
to so many spiritual seekers.

Her energies are clear and uncompromised,
beneficial to all, even those who don't recognize them,
even those who wish to suppress them.

We are delighted you are coming.
Go deep within during your stay.
We will be with you,
indeed have called you here all of your life.

At last you've heard.

Pitch your tent.
Read.
Meditate.
Write.

All will be given.

See you on the Mountain.

2

Mount Shasta

Summer, 2009

On the Mountain

[For many years, my wife, two children, and I would travel US Interstate 5 from our home in Oregon to my parents' place near Sacramento. Around 60 miles south of the Oregon-California border, the highway hugs the southwestern base of Mount Shasta. I would usually slow a bit and lift my eyes to the snowy summit.

It always seemed majestic, but in those days I didn't know that seekers from all over the world came to the Mountain in search of high truths.

We would drive right by Mount Shasta City, a small town off the highway, not suspecting its potpourri of magic stones, crystal bowls, new age books, health foods, herbs, essences, and guided spiritual journeys.

Later in life, as personal struggles spurred my search for a new understanding, I stopped to explore the area.

During late spring through early fall, the little village hosts a cadre of channelers, clairvoyants, healers, shamans, Tibetan monks, Mayan priestesses, and reincarnated Lemurians.

It took me several years to appreciate Shasta. I began to feel at home there. Once, at an outdoor dinner on the edge of town, a sojourner looked out on the plunging white slopes and asked, "Have you heard the call of the Mountain?"

I considered the question, noting how comfortable I was in this strange setting, among people I'd never met before. Admitting it more to myself than to my dinner companion, I said, "Yes, I have."

After finishing my affairs in Portland, I made a predawn departure from the Oregon chapter of my life, and nearly seven hours later, my Jeep hummed up the highway that climbs the Mountain.

In a warm afternoon breeze, the pines waved like old friends. As I swung around a high curve, a vale of snow and mist rose peacefully to the summit — like the in-breath of an opening heart. About 8,000 feet high, a walk-in campground welcomes visitors in early summer, or whenever the snow gives way.

Nearby, waters from deep inside the mountain rise to a small pool. Sparse bubbles climb slowly to the surface and tumble down a slim creek that tiptoes through the alpine meadows below. Heather blossoms highlight the landscape with light strokes of magenta.

Some native cultures believe the world began here, and a sacred contentedness seems to quiet the thoughts of those who come today.

Knowing the peace of Panther Meadows, I took refuge there after leaving my place in Portland.]

[Saint Germain:]

…Doesn't this feel like home? As indeed it is,
for there'll be no returning to the city apartment.
We woke you early to encourage a timely arrival here.

Let's just say we nudged you, for as they say,
"The thing about spiritual guidance
is that you have to take it."

We are delighted to have you.
Now turn down the lantern
and let the Mountain be your bed.

Sleep well…

…So, how fare you?

For so long you've wanted to come and stay awhile,
to embrace Lady Shasta.
In these blessed energies,
the heart is lighter and more at peace.

Life is a thick fluid of events,
and true progress is slow,
but all brings you here, to this Mountain, this moment.

We've watched, guided,
often seen you far afield of your mission,
but such is the human experience.

One must choose a path,
and there are many choices.

Steps astray lead changed people back to life's mission
with new experience and knowledge.
The choices, good and bad, expand the universe
and offer new potentials for spiritual evolution.
Yours have, for yourself and others.

Let the reverence of the Mountain quiet you.
The forest floor cools to the morning breeze.
Fair-haired moss climbs the pine's ruddy trunk.
Meadow birds chat in the branches above.
A warm blue sky embraces all,
yielding to the golden goodness of the sun.

On this Mountain, in these woods, doing this work,
consider how at home and in harmony you are…

…We're glad you've decided to write this evening.
Here atop the mountain road the lantern's golden light
falls soft upon the page.

In your readings today,
the phrase "Life is growth through experience"
captured your attention.

Well is it not?
We discover the effects we have on others

by experiencing those effects ourselves.
By hurting others, then suffering a similar wrong,
evolving souls learn to abstain from harmful actions,
realizing the pain will return to them.

We learn rightful living through the lessons of karma.
As to whether your experiences are causes –
actions that will eventually return to you –
or effects – the receipt of karmic liabilities –
they are both.

What's given affects what's received,
so offer to others kindness and acceptance.

Ascended beings project unconditional love,
for that is what they enjoy in return,
loving projections echoing back.

Life is growth through experience…

…You awoke today in a mood of forgiveness,
the ultimate capacity of humans
and their ultimate challenge.

So often people feel wronged.
So often life seems unfair.
So often others seem ungrateful,
but they are the center of their universe
as you are the center of yours.

Forgive who you must on Earth.
Your soul follows its course,
and other souls follow theirs.

Once, when you visited the old house
and greeted your wife's new partner,
a friend commented,
"There's nothing like some old-fashioned forgiveness."
He was right.
Nothing could better improve the plight of humanity.

Since the divorce the years have passed,
and time is no small factor in forgiveness.

Awakening in the high forest today,
could you but compare your lifted spirits
to the hurt-filled heart of the days of divorce,
spending that first cold night on the Mountain,
you would marvel with us
at the flexibility, adaptability, and healing capacity
of the human spirit.

The abuse and disappointments of troubled lives
are tough training for developing souls,
and at times even the gods join humans
for a hard dose of mortality.

Stay on the Mountain as long as you wish.
You are our guest here.
More so, this is now your home.
It settles you so.

May you enjoy a life of peaceful knowing.

Ascension

[Saint Germain had much to say about ascension from our current circumstances in the third dimension to the higher awareness of the fifth dimension. Those thoughts are collected here.]

Many consider the third dimension to be
    the only reality,
but those with higher awareness know better.
A dimension is a skill to be mastered,
and all must eventually do so.

I may be able to manifest my presence there,
scoot about the planet, bi-locate, quanti-locate,
speak languages, manifest forms,
and escort souls on journeys to distant realms,
but that is not the type of mastery we seek.

There is more serious work to be done.

The harvest of Earth has come,
and those able to free themselves
will ascend with her to the fifth dimension
for higher levels of spiritual attainment.
Those unable to advance
will begin another cycle of Earth-like civilizations.

Which would you rather do?...

...Ascension is a raised consciousness.
The lifting of the body into the sky is a metaphor.
Seekers do not fly somewhere to meet us;
they raise their consciousness and perceive us,
for we are currently near.

Truly, one never stops ascending until rejoining God.
At that point no sense of separate identity exists;
however, the reunion is so blissful
there is no feeling of loss...

...At the end of your meditation sessions
ask that the energy level remain through the day.
Some spiritual people practice all day long.
Many are cloistered in monasteries or ashrams.
Some are secluded in caves or simple rooms.

You are most like the recluse.
This can be lonely, but it is simple and consistent.
Being exposed to the doubts of others
can weaken spiritual resolve.

Sometimes you jokingly claim to have gone crazy.
Somehow this comforts you, but it isn't true.

You have chosen an independent course
and are ascending from the third to the fifth
        dimension...

…Worries that efforts to ascend
will undermine social responsibilities are unfounded.
Remember, a spiritual advancement is forever,
but social progress on Earth can be taken away.

To build upon their previous spiritual gains,
some souls reincarnate in enlightened families.
Some ascend in the state after death,
without returning for another life.
This should be considered after passing over,
as more is known on the other side.

Some who are now resolved not to return to Earth
will reconsider once they cross over
and see the possibilities of a more peaceful lifetime.

Whatever course they choose,
a steady practice of meditation and stillness
will help your readers ascend,
but they must make time for this.

The world is chattering away at them,
chipping off their days one at a time,
until this opportunity on Earth is gone.

Modern technology captures their attention;
they must free themselves from its hold.
We are not contacted through these outer devices
but through an inner, personal exploration.

Let technology make survival easier,
and use the resulting freedom to seek inner guidance
and a return to the divine status from which we came.

Earth cannot wait for humans.
She is ascending now due to her cosmic position.
Ascend with her…

…Last night, as you began to surface from sleep,
a blue trident took root in your abdomen
and steamed up through your torso.
Then the center prong,
layered with artichoke-like scales,
thrust higher and thicker than the others.

This is your version of a scepter,
for you are not the type to wield a sword.
Use it more as a shield and a source of power,
holding it upright in front of the heart and face
as you advance through the challenges of ascension.

Seekers don't often sense these clandestine events,
but much work is done during the sleep state
with the hope that, during the waking state,
higher energies will emerge into the world of form.

As spiritual people strengthen their innate abilities,
they become more directly aware of these goings-on,
as you experienced last night…

…Not all sense the heavenly host,
but choirs of angels
do indeed accompany a soul's approach
to the source of life,
The Great Central Sun.

While the souls of seekers fly home,
they hear music in adoration of the creator of all.
Every moment near the source cleans the karmic slate.

Never fear to go; never doubt you are worthy.
If your presence feels tentative,
say, "I deserve to be here."
For you do indeed, that is the only way to get there.

When the setting seems to fade to a fragile illusion,
look at something more closely;
observe detail, keeping the larger scene in mind.

You are not imposing on the higher beings;
they wish to steady your stay.
Some will look on when you return to the world
and encourage actions leading to your own ascension.

As people look away from everyday conditions
and sense their founding divinity,
the grip of 3D reality becomes less tyrannical.

Once they live in the higher realms,
they may revisit the everyday world
and help others along the way.

Life's goal is not to succeed in the common reality,
but to ascend out of it…

…Transitions, eternal transitions, such is life.
To clutch or cling is folly.

Tomorrow you leave the Mountain.
We have so enjoyed our talks
along the path to the upper meadow.

The high Mountain energies
have been a spiritual wind at your back.
You also benefit from the cosmic position of Earth
and the help of those who've already ascended.

Please devote your energies to this opportunity;
so many beneficial conditions have come together.
The wind is at your back, but you must lift the sails.
Only your attention, only your work brings you home.

Godspeed and a timely return.

3

Shasta Valley

Autumn 2011 – Winter 2013

In the Valley

[After leaving Shasta, I set aside the channeling and pursued professional and personal goals in the Southeast.

I admire those who maintain a consistent spiritual practice – day after day, year after year – but I tend to be more sporadic and can lose the balance between spirit and material realms. The demands of everyday life preoccupy me and I sometimes feel barely able to hold them together. There seems to be no time for contemplative activities. However, as G once predicted, I always return to them.

Having handled the activities in Florida as best I could, I returned to California and settled into a house in the high desert region northwest of the Mountain.

As I resumed the channeling, the view through my window told of late fall. A chill wind lashed stalks of sage and grass. Worried pines sighed and swayed. Cold weather called, but I was warm and well-provided for as autumn befell the Shasta Valley.]

[Saint Germain:]

You need but write. I'm here.
We've had much to say,
but you've been adrift in the world.

Time has passed since you left Shasta,
and as happens so often, she calls you back.

May I pace the room?
Look out the windows
and recall my time on Earth?

I've let go the physical lives,
but today I remember them with fondness.
Fondness and perhaps an immature wistfulness,
for I know my path is well chosen.

I leave you now to yours…

…We're happy to speak with you this morning.
Our conversations depend on your receptiveness
more than my availability.
At times you look away from our encounters,
and we move on to other activities.
As for our conversations,
the more constancy, the better.

Consider spending more time in meditation.
Once the morning session ends,
the day pulls you away.
Extend the session longer
and benefit from the momentum present.

This pushes other activities into later periods,
but little you do is on a particular schedule.
Since your spiritual focus declines with the day,
the later, less useful activities may be dropped.

You progress beautifully;
your sensitivity to the Shasta energy develops.
It may seem that too little is happening,
but not so…

…Our words are still in your hands.
As a channel, you are a "keeper."

You needn't worry what to write.
Hearing our thoughts is your privilege,
but you don't have to create them.
You need but listen, and we'll speak.

These writings fulfill one of your life goals.
An undeniable desire to come to the Mountain
and a strong appetite for spiritual literature
are signs of support from unseen powers.
So carry on with the work,
in faith that it will serve its purpose.

Seek opportunities to present this material;
at least recognize and consider them.
Try to specify their possible outcomes.

Move forward cautiously (as you usually do)
but do move (as sometimes you do not).

Come back often; we're not done with you…

…Enjoy this time of peace.
The occasional moments of despair pass.
Anger passes. Fear passes.
More often these days you are content.
The current emotional tones bring comfort,
and in the thoughtful quiet,
homeward turns the soul.

By keeping thoughts high, energies bright,
and consciousness enlightened,
you shall rise
and human concerns will fall into place.
Much is left to do, much to learn, much to give;
so please listen more often.
The peace here cannot be found elsewhere,
and time with us deprives you of nothing.

We welcome you back.

The Shasta Valley Lessons

[Often, when beginning a session, I think of a current personal concern or activity. Saint Germain seems content to devote a session to these topics.]

Relationships

Encounters with others are complex and rewarding.
Relationships are valued there,
and sharing experience does seem to substantiate it,
but from here, they are viewed differently.
We consider how they've evolved over lifetimes.

When people feel comfortable together,
they may have met in previous lives.
The familiar vibrations attract them,
and their souls continue their work together.
Sometimes this goes on for centuries.

Develop relationships with strong people,
those who are spiritually evolved.
In giving to them, seek no selfish return,
but enjoy what fruits may come.

Those far along the spiritual path
will affirm your own journey.
Such relationships are adventures.

Yes, some problems arise,
but maturely shaped unions can benefit all.
Look for ways to help others,
and give freely of your energies and resources,
for there will be plenty more available.

Treat others with generosity and compassion;
in so doing, your own life becomes more promising.

Engage others joyfully, never interfering or coercing.
Force does not work,
for their own source of divinity should guide them.

Remember that solo activities are also valid.
Do not demand of others
blessings and support that lie in your own being.

Do good. Help others. Ascend.

Gain and Loss

Instead of considering what's lost,
think of what's offered.
Losses are inevitable;
instability, impermanence, and constant change
are the axioms of Earth life.

Everything is in play;
people make choices and experience the results.

Right decisions lead out of the Earth game
into the higher realms.

A focus on loss dredges up hard emotions:
grief, rebellion, vindictiveness, and resentment.
A focus on gains has better results:
gratitude, contentment, opportunity, and hope.

Gain and loss go on for lifetimes.
Sometimes, a person will dismiss an option
that recalls a bad decision in a previous life.
An attractive course of action
may recall a successful choice made in the past.

Every activity holds the risk of loss
and the chance of reward.
Often the rewards are unexpected,
yet there they are.
Accepting them fosters skillful judgment in the future,
so stay focused on the positive outcomes.

Thankfulness

A thankful attitude serves the grateful.

When they express gratitude for blessings received,
the blessings continue and life changes for the better.

The common sayings, "An attitude of gratitude"

and "Too blessed to stress,"
are true and profound.

In all situations can be found subjects of gratitude,
even the trials, indeed especially them,
for when a struggle is carefully considered,
a lesson emerges.
We all receive our share of both
and should be thankful for them.

Healings

The physical treatments you've been receiving
align the body with its chakras,
opening it to incoming energies
as buried pains and unpleasant emotions are cleared.

The past situations do not improve any,
for they have already occurred,
but the ego's attachment to them diminishes.
They carry less weight,
and the seeker becomes lighter,
more able to rise with the available energies.

Healers sense physical and etheric misalignments,
usually through tensions in the seeker's body,
and work to correct them.
This directs attention to the present moment.

The seeker becomes more comfortable,
more responsive to current conditions,
rather than mired in the past.
Fresh outlooks and new ideas result
as the individual accesses the higher bodies.

The healers themselves are conduits,
gifted in opening others to the divine energies.
Some take on the negativity being cleared
and must be skilled in sending it back to Earth.

You often want to go it alone
and feel that needing assistance shows weakness.
Not so: all on Earth need help, even the helpers.

Effective healers do not encourage dependency:
they enhance the seeker's own abilities
to access positive energies.

Addiction

Set your coffee down and pick up the pen,
and things will go better for us.

Addictions do conflict with spirituality,
some more seriously than others.
Hallucinogens can be particularly deceptive,
for they often permit sensations of higher dimensions.
If those happen to be in the lower astral realm,
fearful experiences may ensue.

Meeting Saint Germain

When users are taken even higher,
they have no sustaining power.
As the hallucinogen wears off,
they are lowered into darker moods.

Those who raise themselves through meditation
return to their beginning state in a higher mood,
more confident of facing life.

Over time, addicts need more of the substance
to achieve less of an effect,
but meditators learn how to sustain themselves
in an elevated awareness.

If drugs truly improved life,
they would unlock inner strength
rather than trigger dependency.

The more the addicts seek contentment
from an external source,
the further they stray
from the internal powers that are their birthright.

You may now return to your morning coffee.
Oh…has it grown cold?

Food

Yes, I'm with you this morning.
I am here and you are clear.
I wish to speak of an important matter.

Food is only necessary to feed the physical form.
As individuals become more spiritual,
their chakras open to universal energies,
and they need less food to sustain themselves.
In very rare cases, those well-arisen in their bodies
live without eating.

I don't suggest living without food,
but often it becomes a substitute
for energies that should be acquired spiritually.
Food becomes an addiction.

Unprocessed raw foods are sufficient;
plants, rice, beans, nuts, fruits.
No animal products are necessary.

The body then has an energy system close to Earth's
and becomes a healthy child of the universe,
a clear lens between the spiritual and physical.

A clean diet, direct from Earth's produce,
helps one ascend.

Money

A common reaction to pursuing ascension will be,
"What am I supposed to do about money?
No one is going to pay me
for repeating how abundant life is.
The bills won't get paid,
The water and electricity will go away,
then the house,
then the food,
then the body itself."

However, those things eventually fade anyway;
meanwhile, we only suggest that your readers
have faith and a more enlightening experience.

Some will want to manifest a robust bank account,
say affirmations for a few weeks,
notice nothing happening
and conclude, "So much for my own power."
But their outlook is too shallow and naïve.
It's not money they want, but freedom from want,
the opportunity to pursue their own goals,
free from constantly performing work for pay.

Pursuing one's spiritual goals is not about money.
It requires an inward search…free of charge.
Money isn't needed so much as internal inquiry.
Strength is found within, not procured from without.

Were one to create a vision of life with their fortune,
and re-visualize it constantly without dollar signs,
they'd be more likely to "create their own reality."

From a financial point of view,
the higher truths seem irrelevant.
Many feel their occupations and incomes define them,
thinking it negligent to pursue a highly spiritual life.
Yet, there are those who do pursue such a life
and gather the material necessities along the way.

People plan a life before they are born
and are usually confident of adequate supply.
Once born, however, some are misled,
and they overvalue external resources.

Right actions, those aligned with the higher self,
will lead to right living,
including a proper relationship with money.

Earth Issues

You ask why we permit Earth to be so desecrated?
Chemtrails, pesticides, pollution,
war, genocide, human trafficking, child abuse,
the list continues, more yours than mine.

Why do you permit them?
What have *you* done to stop any of this?

You prefer to live in peace, as do we.
We focus on the good and shun evil.

Earth will rise to such a vibration
that the abusers will no longer be able to incarnate.
She will bring to the fifth dimension
only those who can follow her.

The forces of fear and greed
will not enslave the human race. They cannot,
for the perpetrators will be disempowered
by the karmic return of their own abusive behavior.
Then they will try more positive approaches to life,
if not now, in future incarnations.

We spent centuries ascending,
somehow overcoming such abuses, and so must you.

Without the work of the good on Earth,
she would already have been destroyed.
Goodness shall prevail.
Striking out in anger or revenge,
succumbing to depression or despair,
these reactions benefit no one.
So carry on with your practice.

We know people are impatient with conditions
    on Earth,
but they have chosen to be there.
Those living can improve the situation
by shifting attention toward a new age.

Viewed from its current circumstances,
the world seems an impossible mess,
but we know the history of the human race.
We know how good life can be,
and we also remember even darker days
when human life destroyed itself
and the planet had to be reseeded.

The current situation is difficult but not hopeless.
As Earth rises to higher levels of cosmic energy,
and lower, darker entities are unable to reincarnate,
a more enlightened humanity will run the planet.

A New Golden Age will emerge.

4

The Violet Flame

2009 – 2013

The Flame

[The Saint Germain material is not the first of my channelings. In 2002, I recorded messages from my Lemurian spirit guides. Lemuria was one of Earth's first civilizations, a large continent in the Pacific Ocean, and I lived many lives there.

In that land, a violet light beamed so high and brightly into the skies it could be seen for a thousand miles. Ruffling and wavering like the blaze of a fire, the magnificent Violet Flame sustained the qualities of love, compassion, and forgiveness for our highly spiritual culture.

Unfortunately, after many centuries, the continent sank into the sea. Though a small group of Lemurians escaped to Mount Shasta, almost all of the remaining population died. The escapees built a civilization in the caverns of the Mountain: Telos.

Some priests also escaped the catastrophe, transporting parts of the flame to several safe locations, including Jackson Peak in Wyoming. Inside the mountain stands an etheric temple. In meditations, seekers are often guided there to stand before a remnant of the ancient flame, soaring sixty feet high beneath a dome ceiling.

There is also a temple in Telos. Aurelia Louise Jones, in her work The Seven Sacred Flames, *describes a circular temple with amethyst walls and floors of lighter and smoother amethyst crystal. The energies of the flame pervade the room. Various tones of violet rays sparkle from the walls, and dozens of fountains splash away, their waters shaded from light magenta to dark purple. Chairs of violet crystal invite visitors to be seated above a small flame enveloping their lower chakras and a ray from above entering their crown chakra.*

Though many seekers today don't know of these locations, they often appeal to their higher selves to invoke the healing powers of the Violet Flame. I usually begin by saying, "I invoke the Violet Flame for myself, my loved ones, and all others."

In times of conflict with another person, I've imagined both of us enveloped in a violet light. This usually quells my stormy feelings, for only a few moments at first, but consistently holding the visualization seems to eventually work things out.

Imagining ourselves standing in a violet fire, and letting it permeate every cell and atom of our bodies, forgives karmic debt. Long-term use of the flame suspends the impending "payback" experiences and frees us to ascend.

Saint Germain has been the keeper of the Violet Flame for nearly 70,000 years. Esoterics have known about it for centuries, but knowledge became more public when G began communications with Guy Ballard on Mount Shasta in the 1930's. Ballard wrote of this experience in his book Unveiled Mysteries *and went on to found the "I Am" Activity.*

Saint Germain's comments to me are presented here.]

…I love to welcome those who have found the Flame,
for it is mine only to share with others.

A violet mist invites me to this meditation room.
A worldly anxiety may smother your spiritual dreams,
but still they simmer, about to steam
from leaves of lavender tea.

The Flame is real, not a metaphor.
Seek it in your meditations.
Let it blaze from uplifted palms and the third eye,
a violet triangle embracing the heart.

Let glimmer the jacaranda glow,
blazing away karmic debts
and lifting thoughts to higher realms.

During the day, radiate its cleansing energies
by imagining an inner violet glow.
This will open the minds and hearts of those nearby
to a desire for the better good of all.

Its changes are subtle,
stealing unnoticed upon the seeker,
so access the Flame consistently.
This later-life discovery
corrects your course and sails you true…

…The dark smoke of centuries of karma
hovers over humans, dims their vision,
stifles their breath, suffocates their spirit.
Experiences with the Violet Flame
lift them above the pollution, into the divine domain.
There is hope and rescue.

People learn that their actions return to them
with the same effects they've had on others,
for ultimately there are no others.

The Flame always burns,
dissipating the desperation of the human condition
and raising devotees into the realms of right action.

May this be so for you…

…For those desiring to ascend,
the Flame offers a focal point,
expanding human awareness
while Earth transitions to a higher dimension.

As on a college cruise for studies abroad,
learners study the culture of their destination,
and when the ship arrives,
step onto a land not quite so unknown.

So it is with the journey to the fifth dimension.
Seekers study it aboard planet Earth

as she aligns with the central galaxy.
More evolved beings emerge from their study,
more adept at spirituality,
more prepared for the transition.

So live close to the Flame.

Use it daily, as regularly as food,
and it will clear the obscuring thoughts
of everyday consciousness.

Now on with the work...

...Your visions are beautiful,
as though you are a radiant butterfly.
A crystalline flash blazes your body away.
Wings of hot pink flare and smolder into violet tips.

Bathed in this vibrant light,
you are indeed healed and transformed,
growing brighter by the day
as the karmic burdens clear...

...The violet blaze is not an Earthly fire,
consuming oxygen and fuel, but more a focal point
of the forgiving energies of the higher realms,
for we know the darkness humans wander.

We see the downward spiral
of selfish and petty concerns
befalling even the innocent,
even the kind,
even the strongest of spirits.

So we focus our loving, forgiving energies
as a magnifying lens concentrates sunlight.
Love and forgiveness, the highest spiritual energies,
give off a violet glow,
the highest visible frequency.

In the peaceful glow of the Flame
you'll sense the presence of others.
More will gather
as Earth aligns with the central galaxy.

The Flame will lift their hearts higher,
through the ceiling of humanness
into the skies of Godliness.

When seekers come to the Flame,
as someday come they will,
and light their auras with forgiving energies,
a violet dawn
will embrace the skies of the fifth dimension,
and the harvest of humanity will step forward.

The Order of the Violet Flame:
Talks and Teachings by Saint Germain

[The original channelings began with just G and me near the writing desk, but once I began researching the Violet Flame, he sometimes appeared in a different setting. Somewhere in the spiritual ethos is an Order of the Violet Flame, and I was often swept to its meeting place in my meditations. The Order has an outdoor arena similar to a Greek theater. A semi-circular stage looks out on rising granite ledges used for seating an audience.

At times the area is used informally, as members cluster on the seats and stage for small group activities, and it was in this setting I was introduced to the Order. Sometimes on the stage, I seemed to be working on my energy presentation; violet hues flared like butterfly wings from a shaft of crystal white light that embraced my body. When I'd attain the right balance for a few moments, I'd hear some affirmation from small clusters of people casually gathered in the seats. They'd chant a word that sounded like "asana."

On other occasions Saint Germain addressed a full, attentive audience from the stage, and I was privileged to attend. He was easily seen and heard, though there were no lights or microphones. Usually he drifted to his right side near the front of the stage, no beard or mustache, but bushy gray hair and a weathered face creased with experience and wisdom. His dress was casual, a light gray pullover shirt, collarless with long sleeves. He spoke in a reasonable, relaxed and dignified tone, as one who knows the strength of his presentation lies in the message.]

Thank you all for joining us today,
for it is your ceremony, yours and all humanity's,
all tribes, nations, races, genders, and philosophies.

We address not only those living,
but all who have ever lived,
for some are awaiting new incarnations
and are not present on the planet at this time.

Serve them all we do.
We are not intimidated by their numbers,
but gladly challenged by the opportunities before us.

Even so, your individual presence matters.
God considers every story,
for it evolves like no other.
He ignores none, casts none aside,
loves each as his own children,
just as a great composer cherishes every note
of every instrument of every symphony.

Yes, an orchestra of players
turns a melody more grandiose,
but only when the performance of each musician
is inspired and capable.

We say this not to pressure you,
to make you squirm like music students
who've not practiced their parts.
We simply acknowledge your individual role
in the return of humanity to its divine origins.

May the theme of your life
beam high above the orchestra
like the maestro's violin.
When the melody note sings true,
other players hear and align their instruments.
The same is true of the softest plunk of the bass.

Never underestimate the value of your presence,
the relevance of your story.
Live as though you matter, for so you do…

…Namaste my friends,
greetings to all and each of you

Your gathering here is more dynamic
than your individual efforts combined,
just as a hundred logs together
blaze brighter than one at a time.

The synergy intensifies the power of the Flame,
and extends it further into humanity,
calling more souls to us.

So your individual work is important,
but so are these gatherings.

This evening, I've come again to encourage you,
in moments of wondering what to do,
to return here and warm the hands and heart.

Treasure these violet flares
from your palms, heart, and forehead,
for sensing them with your spiritual sight
brings you more fully to our presence.

Accept the forgiving energies
as the wick yields to the candle's fire,
for true understanding of actions past
removes the need for future events
that would be the karmic reaction.
Once the past and future balance,
karma ceases and the soul no longer suffers
the cycles of birth and death.

Rather, all affected rise
on a tide of forgiveness and divine rejuvenation
into the fifth dimension,
unshrouded by the shortcomings of the past
and the impending paybacks of the future.

So in your meditations come here often,
to this gathering place of those seeking the Flame.

In this life, or any future life,
no progress made here is lost.
The Violet Flame transcends time
and weakens the grip of the lower dimensions.

All here may balance the karmic liabilities
of lives past and present
by giving and receiving forgiveness…

…Welcome back to this ceremony of the Sacred Flame.

Each of you has a distinct electronic frequency
that rings true in the higher dimensions.

When together you project the Violet energies,
the universe acknowledges
the lifting momentum of Earth
and celebrates its blossoming awareness.

Leave aside your worldly concerns,
for they often suppress spiritual inclinations.
Call upon your higher selves
to invoke the Violet Flame.
Not only are we of the higher realms gratified,
but Earth improves as well.

You may wonder, "Is it real?"
Are you only imagining the Violet Light,
this gathering, me speaking?
To borrow a term from the artists,
this ceremony is surreal, above real.

You break no rules by coming here,
you lose nothing, offend no one.
Everyday living remains subject to everyday rules,
but you agreed to those.

You see, once players walk on a field,
they comply with the regulations of the game.
There will be winners and losers,

but those playing have another life,
be they school children soon called to dinner
or professional athletes soon to leave the field
and return to their homes.
Some take the game more seriously than others,
but it is not all of their existence.

Nor is Earth life all of yours.
So play a good game,
then walk off the field
and enjoy returning to your loved ones here.
Your next game will be better for it.

Joy to you…

Signing On for Service

[During my visits to the Order, a guide was consistently at my side, offering some orientation to the activities. She once took me to a building similar to a university library with Greek columns and marble stairways.

As we entered the vestibule, she guided me to a smaller room with a wood podium that served as a platform for a massive book, opened to parchment pages. On the stand, slightly above the tome, sat an old black inkwell from which stood a dip-style pen, round – where my fingers would hold it – but tapered to a tip at the top.

I was expected to sign a commitment, but as I brought the pen to the parchment, just signing my everyday name didn't seem appropriate. I intuited the name Ramulus, not certain I got it exactly right, but close.

Then my guide walked me back to the arena and I found myself on stage with Saint Germain. We stood before a full audience of members of the Order as G addressed me directly.]

You have signed into our library as Ramulus...so be it.
Use it in our Order, for its reputation precedes you.
As to everyday life, use the name as you wish.
When a person uses an etheric name,
others sometimes object,
feeling pressured to accept the accompanying beliefs,
but force is not the way of our Order.

Listen to my words and record them.
Present the message to the best of your ability.

[Saint Germain then introduced me to the audience]:
Please welcome Ramulus, to whom we offer,
and from whom we expect, good work.

[I began speaking to the group]:
I am Ramulus. I greet you…

[After considering some gendered terms, I said…]:
I greet you, dear ones.

[Concerning my relief to have found the right words, Saint Germain counseled]:
Don't worry what words to say.
When the time comes, so will the words.

So be it and welcome to the Order of the Violet Flame.

Teachings

[Sometimes Saint Germain would address small groups with specific teachings. Those that I attended are presented here.]

What is teaching?
The more advanced reach back
and offer a hand to the less advanced.
This is so in the schoolroom as well as our work here.

If, on the way to the summit,
I have come to a difficult cliff
and managed my way to the ledge above,
I may delay my climb
and to those following behind
point out the footholds one-by-one.
This is more fruitful than turning my back
and racing higher.

We are all scaling the heights.
As others have said before,
the work, the glory, the achievement
is on the mountainside, not the summit.

When we climb a mountain, we believe there is a peak.
When we work with higher entities,
we believe there is a highest one.

As we are guided, we guide others up,
to the highest of all.

The Divine Pilot Light

Good to see you all so soon again.
Let's speak of God within today.

Imagine a great sun
with countless rays projecting outward,
every person the advancing point of their own ray.

Looking within their hearts,
they discover this tip of light
and the warmth of the Central Sun embraces them.

This core divinity, like a divine pilot light,
flickers in the hearts of all,
and to us the human race sometimes seems
a galaxy of stars lighting a dark and troubled night.

The true purpose of human life
is to discover this internal divinity
and project it into the world of form.

Never forget the God presence harbored within;
it is a treasure and a responsibility.

Religions often pose God as someone outside
awaiting an invitation,
someone whose companionship must be earned
through certain behaviors and attitudes.
To an extent this is true,

but the divine presence is already inside,
already loving you.
Can't you feel it?

By finding and applying their internal spiritual power,
brought from the time before birth,
those concerned with Earth's direction
will be able to right her course.

Hardly anyone there appreciates
how dire the need is.
We say this not to frighten;
enough fear disturbs the people.

So many are afraid of reprisals,
so many live in denial,
so many have given up,
so few seem aware of anything
but the material substance around them.

But fed with the flow of heavenly energies,
the divine pilot light will expand and blaze
into a brighter, warmer fire,
and the glow therefrom will guide the seeker home.

Mystic Experience

Thank you all for coming.
Let's discuss the special experiences you're having.
They are to be treasured.

These energies tapped in your meditations,
these beings you encounter,
these mystical scenarios,
these rushes of love,
these blissful delicacies of spirit,
build your capacity to navigate the heavens.
Explore them with faith and trust.

Yes, be careful in your etheric journeys.
Yes, protect yourselves.
Yes, "Do unto others...."
But yes, explore as well.

Do not turn away,
saying, "So what? How does this help me
in a world that recognizes only the tangible?"

That is the world's problem, not yours.
Those who know better are blessed,
for the tangible world is diminished
when viewed from the open skies of bliss.

Returning to Earth

Some ask if they can balance karmic debt here
and never return to Earth.

That's a yes and a no.
It may not be necessary
for the spiritually advanced to return,
but they may look back with compassion
on those still smothered under the Earthly shroud.

How can the compassionate ones help
unless attention is directed Earthward?
Earth is so fine, a kind and devoted mother,
but her humans are a problem.
Were they as devoted to serving each other,
would you resist returning?

There *can* be a New Golden Age
if the work of the enlightened
guides the efforts of those less privileged.

Some complain that physical survival
forces collaboration with the unenlightened.
Well...again...yes and no.

People, to put it simply, acquire more than they need.
Sellers trap buyers into future purchases.
The self-centered trap the gracious
into unwise commitments.

Seekers must shield themselves from these abuses.
They must look instead to Earth for provision.

We know of the disappointments
with your human family,
but entreat Mother Earth, not the in-laws.
She will be generous.

Sharing Spirituality

Many feel spiritual studies have little practical value.
Seekers return to the world,
to their jobs, their problems, their culture's problems,
and are unable to maintain an uplifted consciousness.
The unenlightened surround them;
and many will not even discuss spirituality.

As with any joy in life,
spiritual people want to share their experiences,
but others stifle such attempts,
as though these activities are a threat,
and the joyful descend into silence.

Asked about day-to-day interests,
they give acceptable answers,
not mentioning a spiritual fire blazing within,
adjusting thousands of years of karmic imbalance.

They do not discuss their etheric visions,
as exuberant as these experiences may be.
In rejoining the world, seekers go to their corners
and plod away at jobs and responsibilities.

But shouldn't the pursuits here
be influencing those everyday activities?
More to the point, don't they?

Being good to associates,
following the Golden Rule,
carrying an inner joy and a violet glow
does affect the world.

It is not necessary to speak of mystical events,
thereby making others uncomfortable;
goodness speaks for itself.

There is no need to withdraw or hide;
meet others where they are and treat them well.
Share goodness, offer help,
and maintain an uplifting approach to relationships.
That is more important
than the details of personal beliefs.

Hold a strong spiritual presence
and respect the souls of others.

Balance

Strive to balance the worldly and the spiritual.

It's not always wise to pursue one course of action
to the exclusion of another.

Leaving your professions, for example,
to concentrate more on spiritual activities
may not be necessary or even desirable.

Going without resources for worldly survival
can divert attention from spiritual endeavors.
Many have chosen those renunciations,
but if they are not chosen,
spiritual seekers will be distracted.

Some feel that, unless some options are eliminated,
the alternatives will not be taken,
but this is not necessarily so.
Opportunities cannot be forced to appear,
they must be recognized and then pursued.

The next step always comes
from where the feet now stand.
Leaving something behind
must be decided case-by-case.

Seek the proper balance.
Plan yet trust.
Be realistic yet intuitive.

Keep your own life in order while helping others.

If you must focus on the next step, so be it.
If the next path,
the next horizon,
the next dimension,
so be it.

The Word "God"

Let's speak of the word "God" today.
Not the word of God, the word "God,"
which is often associated with religions
that want to control and judge.

That is not God's way;
nonetheless, many will not tolerate the term,
trying to distance themselves from such oppression.

Some refer to the highest power as Source or Spirit,
non-personalized terms, non-gendered as well,
addressing the concern of saying "He" and not "She."

God encompasses both the masculine and the feminine,
just as humans bear the traits of both genders
and have lived lives as men and women.

Regrettably, terminology polarizes people,
often preventing any further discussion;
however, that does not mean we should be silent.

Language is not the truth to which it points,
so I will use my own terminology
and permit others to use theirs.

God is an ocean
in which we swell with the winds
and recline with the calm.
We are a splash on the waves,
able to visit distant shores
and remote regions of the seas.

I live in service to God.
It is the path down which I carry my lamp.
Should any wish to follow,
I will pause and light the ground before them,
and as they move forward,
so will my light.

As always, I am yours in God.

Prayer

How does one pray?
What should one pray for?
So few know this simple concept.

A prayer is an appeal, a beseeching, a noble wish
for the realization of one's highest intentions,
an articulation of one's finest desires
in hopes of manifesting them.

The angels themselves cannot dismiss prayer.
They must respond.
Demons cringe, impotent in the presence of prayer.
They must defer.

It carries such power, yet so few pray.
In thirst they stumble on dusty stones
when water flows beneath the ground.
They need but dig down
and pull the wellsprings to their lips.

How trustingly children kneel at a bedside
and ask God to bless their mommies and daddies.
How believing and intent they are.

What becomes of these children?
God has not stopped listening,
has not looked away,
but with age they turn elsewhere
and make appeals to an uncaring world.

Pray for others as well as yourself,
remembering it is not you helping them,
but their own inherent divinity
awaiting their attention.

Ask that they turn inward and follow its guidance.
Do not give up wanting a better world.
Appeal for, and be thankful for,
any measures that bring it closer.

Pray often.
Pray hard.
Pray.

Now good night my friends.

Say your prayers and off to bed.

"Unforgiveable" Actions

All sensitive people have regrets
and are especially mortified to have hurt someone
and be unable to mitigate the injury.
I could give examples,
but those of you involved in such an incident
know all too well what I mean.

Evolved people want to mend
any damage they've caused others,
but some of these events
cannot be adequately addressed in this lifetime.

Sometimes, dealing with them at the Earthly level
only makes the situation worse,
and the resulting karma could bind one
for lifetimes to come.

Hearts are troubled by these trials,
for the stains of such messes seem so permanent.

These are some of the hardest lessons of life.
For these situations that cannot be remedied,
appeals should be made to the higher levels.
We recommend clearing the debt
by bringing the circumstances to the Violet Flame.

We also recommend prayer,
for only with faith can one seek unseen solutions.
Seek the Violet Flame.
Pray sincerely.
Accept what love may come from others.

At least be comforted in knowing
that such occurrences are an instructive part of life;
they teach what not to do,
and your concerns result from respecting others
and caring about how you've treated them.

Hiding inside your worldly personality,
becoming needlessly busy and productive
as a means of distraction from these issues,
only lets them fester
in the darkness of the subconscious mind.

They should be addressed at the spiritual level.

We are always here for you,
especially in the moments of despair.

Personal Devastations

All lives have their share of personal devastations.
Yes, they seem unfair, and those involved in one—
a loss, a betrayal, an injustice, an injury or death—
have my compassion.
Some suffer for an unknown duration,
wondering when the hurting will stop.

Indeed the clouds may mask any hope of sun,
and as happens in some climes,
cold and windy rains
may be forecast for months to come.

I've lived many lives on Earth.
I have a more enlightened perspective now,
but that doesn't assuage your turmoil.
I know this.

So often, as a soul leaves for Earth,
we of the spirit realms step back
with respect and concern for the upcoming challenges.
The soul knows of them but goes anyway.

Seen from this perspective,
life's tribulations are not unfair.
You chose them. They will strengthen you.

Your lives are stories.
Did you know that those of other dimensions
observe your trials,

learning the lessons with less emotional havoc
than living through the struggles would require?

You endure these personal disasters
not only for your own advancement
but for that of others as well.
Will they pity you, praise you – bless you
for an inspirational response to the challenges of life?

Just as you arose this morning,
however dreading the day ahead,
arise again tomorrow morning, and the next.

You are not a worthless castaway of human experience
but the protagonist of a unique tale.
Remember those of the higher realms
who want to know the outcome of your struggle.

Lift them up.

Suffering Abuse

The world in general does not reward
those who follow the Golden Rule,
keep personal commitments,
and obey moral principles.

Too often their worldly reward
is abuse by those who scoff at such standards,

or who outwardly proclaim right action
and secretly behave otherwise.

And so the good are stunned and hurt,
bewildered by the selfishness of the offenders.
Yet the evolved response is of course not vengeance,
but quiet acceptance.

"Vengeance is mine saith the Lord"
is not the warning of a wrathful God,
but an affirmation of the laws of karma:
what one sends out, one receives back.
You needn't do anything
to help along this fundamental principle of life.

Certainly these insults and affronts can incite anger,
but withhold retaliation, not out of cowardice,
but in respect for others.

Others have done so for you.
They have withheld their anger
and permitted you to recognize your disrespect later,
perhaps on the receiving end of a similar affront.

Parents, when hurt by the thoughtlessness
of the children they love so much,
often recall being as inconsiderate
of their own parents.

So they endure the affront in silence
or express how the child's behavior makes them feel,
and leave the returning effect to karma.

Even though hurt and unsatisfied with a situation,
you are not aware of all the karmic circumstances,
some from previous lives: theirs, yours, or both.

Tell yourself, "It seems unfair but I must endure this."
Becoming vindictive and hateful
only degrades your own life.

Belief in karmic justice is an element of faith.
The sufferer does not see the fairness
but believes it somehow exists.

Other spiritual beliefs are this way.
Faith precludes rational proof;
it accepts truths outside the domain of the rational.

If explanations are clearly present,
wherein lies the faith?

If you do believe in karmic balance,
wherein lie the damages?

I remember angry times in my own lives,
thinking such advice was for the weak and gullible,
but this is not so.

Though we are all bound for the heavens,
some are further along than others
and will suffer the abuse of those less advanced.

I hope this has helped.
The resentments of life
are a hard knot in the heart
that must be diligently and thoughtfully untied.

So trust your beliefs, play by the rules,
and leave the rest to providence.

Bless you all dear ones, come back often.

Fear

What is fear
but reluctance to pursue an experience,
an attempt to predict and avoid pain and discomfort?

Sometimes fear points to what you should be doing,
but afraid of reprisals,
you don't follow your intuition,
even though it may be better founded than the fear.
Intuition comes from the higher self,
which exists in a fearless state.

Following your instincts may pave the way forward,
nudging aside the anticipated obstacles and reprisals.

When you do encounter a crisis,
the higher self will come forward,
alertness will increase,
you'll identify the critical details of the situation
and overcome threats in surprising ways.

So don't underestimate your ability
to prevail over the anticipated difficulties;
they often symbolize the challenges
you have stepped on Earth to confront.

Works

When humans began to solicit outward experience,
rather than create it,
they became enamored with themselves.

Instead of the noble sentiments of their hearts,
they manifested forms that might reward them.

Then, in preference to "looking upon the world
and seeing it was good,"
they wanted others to tell them so,
to reward them with recognition, respect, payment.

From there, it was "Let the games begin!"
Individuals tried to outdo each other.

Jealousy, envy, and resentment resulted.

Instead of being creative, humans became self-serving
and aggressive toward others.

Where was the fork in the road?
When they sought external approval
rather than valid self-assessment of their own divinity.
This haunts them still.

"And God looked upon the world
and saw that it was good."

"And God looked upon the world
and called his agent
to see if anyone might possibly finance it."

"And God looked upon the world
and fretted that it might offend someone."

How absurd those last statements are,
for God as well as you.
God hopes you'll create a good world of your own.

Create from your heart, not the expectations of others.

The true purpose in sensing heavenly qualities
is to bring them to Earth.

Your Life Mission

My friends we meet again.
Today, I speak of a certain kind of peace.
It levels the turbulent currents, slows the flow,
and deepens the river's channel.

Deep waters, low and slow, found a peaceful surface.
So use meditation to dive within yourselves.
Splash through the roiling surface,
then go down to the quiet waters.

The malleable circumstances of the world
are but a venue for the free will,
a medium for the soul's work.

Your life is a work of art,
the world a palette and brushes
used to express the vision with which you were born.

So retrieve the founding dream.
Then arrange the forms, shadows, colors, tones, lights,
and abstractions of the world
to manifest your vision.

Consider your life.

Do you like it?

Are you at peace with it?

May you answer these questions
as the artist who regards the canvas and says,
"Yes! That is what I saw, what I wanted to portray."

Great artists do not just play with their talent,
but shape their medium
to portray a profound personal vision.

Serious people do not just juggle events
in clever, self-serving ways,
but pursue their original mission,
live the life they dreamed before birth.

"Yes," they say, "this is why I came here.
What I wanted to experience and accomplish."

Painters first have a vision and then they paint.
Souls have a mission and then begin a life.

Artists sometimes wonder
if a project should ever have been attempted,
if it's going to fail,
how it will ever be finished,
but somehow the work gets accomplished.

Not always completely satisfied,
a better artist emerges from the challenge.
This is also so with human lifetimes:
a better soul emerges.

Induce your life to reflect its original mission,
a gem found in the depths of the meditating mind.
Then will you find peace.

I leave you to your work.

Closing Comments

[Saint Germain gives the closing address to a general meeting of the Order]:

You've all come in common purpose,
to spread the Violet energies on your planet
and let them glow in the universe.

Lift your minds from the problems of the world
and feel with us tonight the loftiness of the Flame.
The world can be healed, it must be.
The required powers are here for you
to invoke, treasure, and promote through your auras.

Persevere and the presence of the Violet Flame
will be undeniable by anyone on Earth.

You are the pioneers
who will settle Earth's new frontier,
the fifth dimension.
Others will follow, but for now, pioneer.

You'll have your share of head-shakers and naysayers,
but remember who has the doubt and who the vision.
Take no counsel of the doubts. Consult your vision
and that of other's looking to the dimensional shift.

Lift Earth to heaven
since so few want to bring heaven there.

Gather here as you've often done.
Support each other,
however ethereal the relationships,
however lonely you may feel in your bodies.
Come here and invoke the Flame together.

You are not alone,
and as the fifth dimension manifests on Earth,
a New Golden Age will begin.

You'll embrace one another with real arms,
recalling the friendships of many lifetimes,
joyful as children at play.

Until we meet again my friends.

Namaste.

5

Afterword

December, 2012

The Book

{During the stay in Shasta Valley, I continued the sessions with Saint German and organized the transcripts of the past few years into book form, a work I eventually titled Meeting Saint Germain.*]*

[Saint Germain]:

Thank you for the work on our book.
Make it a part of your daily routine
and it will gather momentum,
just as the meditations and channelings have.

These writings join other efforts of the masters
to help seekers ascend to the fifth dimension.

So you must apply yourself,
make the pages presentable, and then present them.
This takes time, patience, dedication, and courage.

This work, though it points to a higher realm,
is still something outside of the readers;
they will also need to look inward.

At best, they will hear from our words
the connecting click of truth and the human mind.
"That's true," they will silently agree.

All have spiritual origins,
and the click of truth
is the memory of their divine beginnings
so many centuries and lifetimes ago.

Continue to use your time by the Mountain wisely.
Once the book is done, things will become clearer,
so work away, my busy friend.
As Earth approaches the Central Sun,
our message will become irresistible…

…Think of our new age as parallel to the Christian era.
We're just beginning our 2,000 years.
Christianity began as a small group of sincere believers
in an essentially unknown religion,
but it's time had come.

Earth was flooded with Christ-like energies,
souls incarnated to develop them,
and the world changed.
So it will be in the New Golden Age.

You've chosen to incarnate early on
and review some of our principles.
Some spiritual literature has survived for centuries
but its acceptance usually takes time –
time and confirmation from other sources.
Hopefully these ideas will be acknowledged
as higher sensibilities become more widespread.

Consider the young people.
Many are open to spiritual ideas,
comfortably dismissing the common Earth mentality.
As they promote the momentum of truthful living,
the world will change.

So, have faith and diligence in presenting this work,
even if it isn't accepted until far in the future…

…The writing goes well, the book develops,
and your life stream clears.

These communications are supplemented
by a wealth of cosmic energies flooding Earth.
You incarnated knowing they would be available.

In choosing a West Coast life,
you were almost certain to find Shasta,
where the higher energies are intensified.
The Mountain is a major destination of your lifetime.

Don't worry that this work comes too late in life
or too late in the advent of the new era.
Yes, some preparations have already been made,
but consider today's world:
there is still much to do.

Through the windows, view the peaceful landscape.
Fall's end turns the chilly desert inward.

Pines and sage breathe the cool air
and brace themselves for the coming winter.
Earth knows what to do,
but people wonder about timing.

Once they look within and find their personal divinity
the time is right.

Postscript

[During late fall of 2012, the book had taken general form, but it lacked a closing statement. I could think of no better place to channel one than high atop the road that climbs the Mountain, ending near the trailhead to the upper meadows.

While I was driving up, the road faded into a low gray cloud, and the sun seemed to be lost for the morning. But not so. Soon the Jeep rose above the enshrouding mist. At the highway's end, boulders – strewn by the volcanoes and avalanches of centuries past – steamed in the sun. The surrounding buttes jutted through airy vapors fading into a clean blue sky. I was in the light.]

[Saint Germain:]

Don't underestimate our readers.
They have centuries of lifetimes to call upon,
and at their fingertips are streams of knowledge
about me, the higher self, the Violet Flame,
and the process of ascension.

They can also simply read our pages,
and patiently wait for the concepts to surface,
passing through their own low clouds
into the sunshine above.

It may help them to know
that I once walked the Earth as they do now.

Through God's grace and my own efforts,
I ascended out of the 3rd dimension.

I am now dedicated to lifting their souls
as Earth sails the higher energies of the universe.
This mission is far more important
than any recognition I receive.

The concept of a higher self
holds that God lives within us
and should be sought there.

We are the only ones
who can find God within ourselves,
and we must make the effort.

This is usually done through stillness:
meditation, contemplation, prayer,
a presence in nature –
activities muting the noisy concerns of everyday life.
"Be still and know."

The Violet Flame is an energy of the higher realms
that forgives and clears karmic debt.
The readers need but imagine themselves
standing in the center of a violet fire,
the flames surging and ruffling
beneath, through, around, and above them.

As they do, negativity will clear.
Given enough time and concentration,
this activity will lift their spirits
and they will want to know more.

To the readers let me say directly,
we do not prefer this author over you.
You are just as loved by us, just as favored.
All must ascend, and eventually all shall.

I am Saint Germain.
You have my prayers, the Violet Flame,
and all the help I'm permitted to offer.

That is not enough, however.
You must meet my support
with your individual efforts to ascend…

Benediction

May these words fall like rain
on the river that sweeps
all souls to the sea.

— Saint Germain

www.ingramcontent.com/pod-product-compliance
Ingram Content Group UK Ltd.
Pitfield, Milton Keynes, MK11 3LW, UK
UKHW041945230426
12048UKWH00008B/139